D1610268

9999 085 959 0 155 C9

BLECHINGLEY

BY

UVEDALE LAMBERT

SURREY ARCHÆOLOGICAL SOCIETY

THE CLAYTON MONUMENT (1705) IN THE CHURCH

BLECHINGLEY

A Short History

BY

UVEDALE H. H. LAMBERT

GUILDFORD
SURREY ARCHÆOLOGICAL SOCIETY
1949

SURREY LOCAL HISTORY COMMITTEE

A. W. G. LOWTHER, F.S.A., *Chairman.*

T. E. C. WALKER, *Hon. Editor, Local History.*

J. H. HARVEY, *Hon. Secretary, Local History.*

The Committee here records its indebtedness to the following for their assistance in the preparation of this volume:

C. C. FAGG

W. HOOPER, LL.D., F.S.A.

B. RACKHAM, C.B., F.S.A.

J. WILSON-HAFFENDEN.

For all information regarding the Local History Series, apply to John H. Harvey, Half Moon Cottage, Bookham, Leatherhead, Surrey.

All other enquiries should be sent to the Hon. Secretary, Surrey Archæological Society, Castle Arch, Guildford, Surrey.

CONTENTS

THE ILLUSTRATIONS

⊠ ⊠

ACKNOWLEDGMENTS

Thanks are due to Mr. L. F. Salzman and the National Buildings Record for the use and loan of the Victoria County History church plan.

The photographs of the church are by John Maltby and that of Pendell Court is by Windsor-Spice Ltd.

AUTHORITIES

AUBREY, J. *Natural History and Antiquities of Surrey*, vol. III (1719).

ESDAILE, K. A. *English Church Monuments*, 1510-1840 (Batsford, London, etc., 1947).

GOVER, J. E. B., etc. *Place-Names of Surrey*. (English Place-Name Society, vol. XI, Cambridge U.P., 1934).

LAMBERT, UVEDALE. *Blechingley—a parish history*, 2 vols. (1921).
Reference should be made to this for detailed sources.

SURREY ARCHÆOLOGICAL SOCIETY. *Surrey Archæological Collections*, 49 vols. (1858-1946).
Refer to general indexes for vols. I-XXXVIII, and to the following items in later volumes: XXXIX (Parliamentary Representation); XLI, XLIV (Pilgrims' Way); XLIII, p. 44 (Clayton Monument); XLVI, p. 116 (Parish Register transcripts); XLVIII, p. 144 (Enclosure).

VICTORIA COUNTY HISTORY. *Surrey*, vol. IV (1912).

FURTHER READING

GEOLOGICAL SURVEY: *The Geology of the Country round Reigate and Dorking* (1933).

HAWKES, C. F. C. *Old Roads in Central Hampshire* (The Harroway), in *Proceedings Hants Field Club*, vol. IX, pt. 3 (1925).

HEARNSHAW, F. J. C. *The Place of Surrey in the History of England* (1936).

MONEY, B. E. *Queen Anne of Cleves and Blechingley; John Evelyn and Blechingley; Viscount Palmerston and Blechingley* (Pamphlets).

SMITH, E. *The Reigate Sheet of the One-Inch Ordnance Survey* (1910).

WHIMSTER, D. C. *The Archæology of Surrey* (1931).

NOTES in the text enclosed in square brackets thus [D.6] refer to the folding map at the end of the book.

Chapter I

GEOLOGY

It is, perhaps, fitting that we should begin an account of Blechingley by a brief survey of the parish geologically.

The parish of Blechingley is about $4\frac{1}{2}$ miles in length from north to south, and within this short distance it traverses no less than nine geological outcrops—sands, clays and limestones—which give to the parish its delightful variety in relief and vegetation. To the north, in the parishes of Chaldon and Caterham, the bold escarpment of the North Downs overlooks Blechingley. Two bastions of the Downs actually enter the parish in the north-east corner. Paradoxically, the most easterly of these Chalk hills is named Gravelly Hill. This is because it is capped by an outlying remnant of Blackheath Pebble Beds.

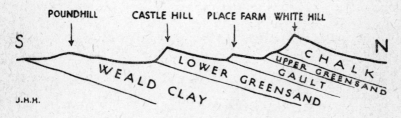

GEOLOGICAL SECTION OF BLECHINGLEY

From beneath the Chalk older formations crop out successively towards the south, their outcrops stretching from east to west across the two to three miles width of the parish. First the Upper Greensand forms a minor escarpment feature at the foot of the Downs on the east side, crossing the parish boundary northwards on the west side. Next, sloping towards the lower ground of the Vale of Holmesdale, the Gault Clay, half a mile in width, extends across the parish from North Park Farm to Warwick Wold and Oakley. The outcrop of the sandy Folkestone Beds, a mile in width, occupies the lower parts of the Vale of Holmesdale (Pendell 320 feet, Brewer Street 345 feet) and rises to a height of over 500 feet at Blechingley village. The three other members of the Lower Greensand series—Sandgate and Hythe Beds and Atherfield Clay—crop out on the southward—facing Greensand escarpment. South of the Greensand, as may be seen from Castle Hill, is the broad low-lying area of the Weald Clay, in parts little over 200 feet above sea-level. This clay area, broken here and there by seams of sandstone and limestone, extends for 2½ miles to the southern boundary of the parish and for a further 2 miles beyond to the fringe of the forest ridge of the Central Weald.

Traversing all these geological outcrops from north to south and bisecting the parish is a watershed which divides two major river basins. The streams which flow eastwards from this median line in the Vale of Holmesdale and on the Weald Clay belong to the Eden-Medway basin ; those to the west flow into the river Mole.

So the parish has the main variety of Surrey geological formations with the different scenery and flora which are associated with them. The bluffs of the chalk downs with their yews and wiry grass, the rich vegetation of the gault, and the bracken and gorse of the sand contrast with the thorns and oaks of the wealden forest and give the parish its colourful beauty basking in the sunshine of a steady southern slope.

CHAPTER II

HISTORY

THE NAME probably derives from *blaecan* (Anglo-Saxon, to bleach) and *ley* (a clearing), connecting the parish with the fuller's earth industry which still is carried on at Nutfield, and possibly gave the name of Walking ("fulling")-stead, which is the ancient name of Godstone. But possibly Blechingley preserves the name of some Saxon family, the ley (or clearing) of the sons (ing) of Blaeca. At any rate the "t" is a later addition, introduced by foreigners and perpetuated by civil servants.

PREHISTORIC TIMES. At the north end of the parish, on White Hill, where the North Downs rise to 750 feet above sea-level, are traces of an Iron Age camp.

Much of it has been removed by modern quarrying, but some traces of the ditch can still be seen along the drive of "War Coppice." Just to the north of this runs one of the routes of the great East to West trackway formerly known as the Harroway, and which, stretching from Cornwall to Kent, was certainly in use throughout most of the Iron Age and may have come into being at a still earlier period. Only in recent times did the name Pilgrims' Way become attached to a part of this early route, and, though there is little likelihood of many pilgrims having made use of this track, the name has now become popularised and is likely to remain. What we can see, however, is that the later, Saxon main tracks were north-south routes leading from the Chalk hills to the Greensand ridge and down onto the weald. Pioneer settlers descended from the Downs to make a "pen" (=enclosure, c.f. Pendhill) or clear a "ley" (Blechingley) or build a "ton" (Chevington) or a "ham," and their lines of communication were up and down Common Lane, Sandy Lane, Stychens, Workhouse Lane or North Park Lane. It was a long time before east-west communications mattered. In our own day the main road from Sevenoaks to Guildford jinked almost every time it met a north-south road, as it still does when it meets the road between the North and South Parks by Water House.

ROMAN PERIOD. Next to nothing is known as to the nature of the occupation in this area during Roman times. In 1813 some workmen discovered a wall near Pendell, and it was found to be part of a hypocaust belonging to the heating system of a Roman building; it was, when discovered, full of Roman tiles. The digging was filled in, and there are no details to show if this hypocaust was part of a Roman villa or of a bath building, like the examples found in Surrey at Farnham, Beddington, Cobham (Chatley Farm) and on Ashtead Common.

SAXON PERIOD. Even less is known about our area during the Saxon period, either as regards the first, or pagan, phase (*c.* A.D. 500-700) or of the later period extending down to the Norman Conquest. Some day chance excavations may reveal pagan burials, or possibly the sites of some of the crude huts of the period (as at Farnham and Guildford).

But placed as it is Blechingley could hardly escape entirely the material events of the Saxon period. It is not fantastic to imagine the parish crossed by the paths of such as Sweyn of Denmark, Olaf of Norway, and King Cnut in their struggles for supremacy in England. Perhaps Blechingley saw Alfred, the Confessor's brother, who landed at Sandwich in 1036 with 600 Normans and marched to his death at Guildford, massacred by Earl Godwin and Harold Harefoot. William the Conqueror may have passed by when, after Hastings, he failed in his direct attack on London and turned south. Was it then that de Clare staked a claim to the lordship of Blechingley? At any rate Domesday Book records the damage wrought in Blechingley and Chevington by the Normans.

Nowadays there are no traces of Saxon life in the parish other than names. Chevington, now just a farm, was an older and larger settlement than Blechingley and remained so even after the Conquest, perhaps until the parish of Horne in the south and the two parks were carved out of it.

DOMESDAY BOOK, 1086. Chevington is mentioned first. Blachingelie is held by Richard de Tonbridge of the King. The record then continues: "There is land for 16 ploughs; there were three manors, it is now made into one manor. In demesne [the land the lord kept for himself] are three ploughs, twenty villeins, four bordars, with nine ploughs. There are there seven serfs; fourteen acres of meadow; from the wood forty pigs, from herbage eighteen pigs."

Richard, who had his main castle at Tonbridge, is better known as Richard de Clare, a second cousin by the halfblood of the Conqueror.

For those not versed in the technicalities of Domesday Book a few notes may be of interest. "16 ploughs," the eight-ox plough team could probably only manage something under 100 acres in this soil yearly. Three hundred acres roughly was the area of land the lord of Blechingley kept in his own hand, tilled by his tenants in return for their holdings amounting to some 900 acres, to produce food for his upkeep when he visited Blechingley Castle. Apparently the balance of "4 ploughs" was not cultivated.

Most of the ploughland would be held in *Common Fields*, lord and villein (a man who lived in the vill or village) having one-acre strips in the three Fields. There is no doubt one of the Common Fields was on the land north of the Church down towards Place Farm, with the old trackways of Workhouse Lane and Stichens ("stitches" or "lands") to east and west of it. Here is still retained the field name, "Furlongs"—the furrow long of the old acre strip, 220 yards long and a cricket pitch wide. The second Common Field was probably on the high ground between Hevers and the village, running from the Outwood Lane to the Tilburstow or Rabies Lane, and the third probably was situated on the rich soil by Pendell, the first cultivated area of the parish.

"Bordars" were whole-time servants, possibly specialists like shepherds, pigherds, etc., who held no strips in the Common Fields but had about five acres round their cottage. The serfs were entirely landless, possibly servants of the lord, but occasionally could be as important persons as the miller.

The fourteen acres of meadow, the only enclosed grassland for hay and very precious, would be in the Funk Brook valley which crossed the main road by the Plough Inn but is now mostly piped.

The significance of the pigs is that it was the custom for the lord to take every seventh pig in return for the use of the woodland and wastes, so the sentence means that there was sufficient food (acorns, etc.) for 280 pigs to be turned out in the woods and 98 pigs in the waste.

It is reckoned that the population of Blechingley and Chevington amounted to some 300 souls. It seems probable that at Chevington we have an example of a manor which, for various reasons, tended to be split into several enclosed holdings rather than each tenant holding strips in Common Fields. Names suggest larger holdings, e.g. Stangrave, Garston, Isemongers (Water House), Rabies, Coldharbour, Wych Croft (Underhills) and the two Parks. Horne also was carved out of the Manor, with the odd "horn" of best land which stretches out to the Grinstead road below Newchapel Green. This may partly explain the decline of Chevington as compared to its apparently more backward rival, Blechingley.

PARISH BOUNDARIES. At the time of Domesday it is clear that the parish stretched from the North Downs probably down to the County boundary in the still unpenetrated thickets below Outwood and Horne, the forest of Andred. On the west was Nutfield, and on the east, Walkingstead, a long but far narrower parish. The boundary between Blechingley and Walkingstead was roughly the line of the Roman road on which, in Queen Elizabeth's time, Godstone sprang up: and to this day the houses on the west of the Green are in the Manor of Blechingley.

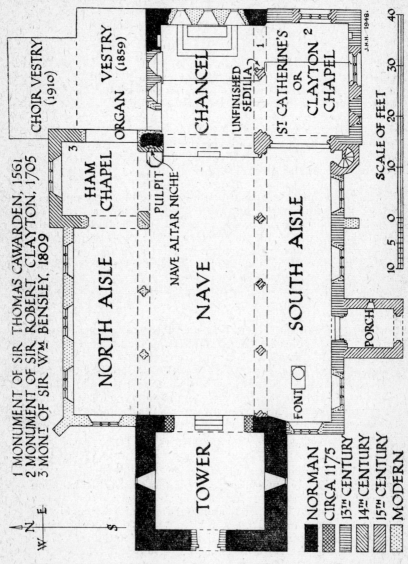

PARISH CHURCH OF ST. MARY THE VIRGIN, BLECHINGLEY: GROUND PLAN

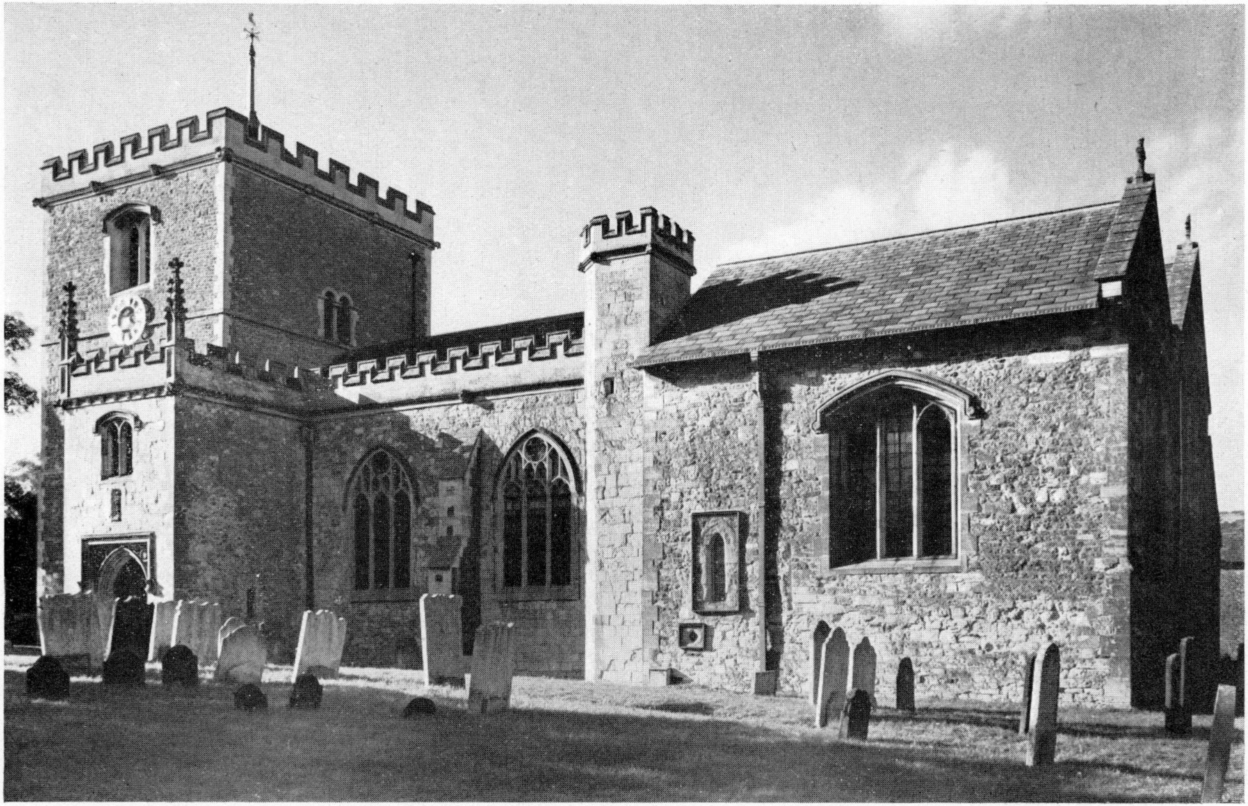

THE CHURCH FROM THE SOUTH-EAST

CHAPTER III

THE CHURCH OF ST. MARY THE VIRGIN

This church is one of the finest in the county, as befits a borough and castle of a great feudal magnate.

THE TOWER is early Norman, about 1090, over 5 feet thick in its lower storey. It was heightened about 1160 by a belfry which had windows similar to that on the east face, and a new arch into the nave was made in the Transitional style. The west door is restored Early English : the window over it dates from the Perpendicular alteration. The battlements are, of course, modern. There used to be a spire which was destroyed by lightning in 1606 which "did in very short time burne the spire . . . and melt to infinite fragments a goodly ring of bells."

THE NAVE. The south arcade of four bays is Perpendicular and the north is modern (1856). The corbels and most of the roof are original.

THE CHANCEL. The chancel arch dates from the Perpendicular alterations made about 1460 by the Duke of Buckingham and his chaplain, Hugh Hexstall, who became Rector in 1451, and altered the whole alignment of the church to fit the new south arcading of that date. At the east the original Early English lancets were replaced by a Perpendicular window similar to that in the south chapel and tower. At the 1870 restoration, Butterfield removed this window and restored three lancets, but neither in shape nor position do they represent the Early English ones. The north arcade of the chancel consists of three Early English lancets (*c.* 1250) and a Norman round-headed window which has given rise to various conjectures, if it is indeed original. The south arcade is wholly Perpendicular. The reredos above the High Altar is by Street (1870) and is notable for the figure of Samuel Wilberforce as Bishop of Winchester put up during his lifetime, among the apostles and saints.

THE SOUTH CHAPEL. The South Chapel is really Early English (*c.* 1230), but much altered in 1460. It was probably dedicated to SS. Catherine and Margaret. Outside on the south wall can be seen blocked lancet windows and a quatrefoil near the ground, and on the inside wall the openings for a door and the two lancets. In all probability this is the remains of the cell of Brother Roger, hermit of Blechingley, who received a grant of a bushel of wheat from Henry III in 1233. It has been suggested that he was a Franciscan, one of the earliest in this country.

THE SOUTH AISLE, again in origin Early English, as the south doorway shows, but much altered in 1460. In the south-east corner the turret and stairway giving access to the rood loft and the windows on the south are Perpendicular, the latter have some good modern glass by Comper, that at the west end of the aisle is by Kempe. The wooden south door itself with its handle, and the porch, date from 1460. Over the porch is a room where our Elizabethan ancestors stored their "harness" against the Spanish invasion. The figure of Our Lady and the Holy Child outside are modern.

THE NORTH AISLE. Entirely Victorian.

THE NORTH TRANSEPT OR HAM CHAPEL, the dormitory of the owners of the Manor of Ham, a detached part of Blechingley in Nutfield, is Decorated work (14th Century). The reformers left a fragment of old glass in the head of the north window.

THE VESTRIES were added in 1859 and 1910.

THE PULPIT. The pulpit was given to the church by Robert Holman, of Pendell, whose arms appear on it with the date, 1630. He was the son of the builder of Pendell Court. The hour-glass stand is contemporary. At the restoration of 1870 this fine Jacobean pulpit was thrown out and removed to Orsett in Essex, whence it was recovered in 1937 and put back in its original place. Behind the back of the pulpit (which can be lifted forwards) can be seen the nave altar niche where no doubt stood the figure of Our Lady as patroness of the church. Some of the original colouring remains.

THE FONT. Perpendicular. The fine oak cover was carved for it in 1906 by Albert Maynard, whose family is reputed to descend from one of Anne of Cleves' retinue.

MONUMENTS. The church is overawed by the vast monument which Sir Robert Clayton put up during his own lifetime, in 1705, in honour of his wife. It is by Richard Crutcher and is considered an excellent example of the work of that period. The fine wrought-iron railings are contemporary and Aubrey recounts that they were painted blue and gold. On the south wall nearby is a tablet to the fifth Clayton baronet, a Waterloo hero.

A marble commemorates Dr. Nathaniel Harris, Rector, 1609-1625, who tried to interfere in the borough elections and had to apologise on his knees at the bar of the House of Commons.

Nearby are commemorated members of the Kenrick family who were closely connected with the parish from the 18th Century to modern times, providing two Rectors and several M.P.'s.

On the south side of the High Altar is the table tomb of Sir Thomas Cawarden, d. 1559. The contemporary brass plate was discovered in 1836 at Loseley, near Guildford, where lived Cawarden's friend, Sir William More, and it was only then put on to the tomb. Sir Thomas was Master of the Revels under four sovereigns, including Henry VIII, and a patron of English drama. He was steward and keeper for Queen Anne of Cleves when she was given Blechingley by Henry on her divorce, and after 1547 he became owner of the Manor. An ardent reformer under Edward VI, he removed the rood and other fittings from the church, but he managed to square his conscience under Queen Mary.

In the north-east corner of the Ham Chapel is a monument to Sir William Bensley, who married the sister of J. S. Biscoe of Pendell House and died 1809. The monument by John Bacon, Jnr., with its ship and elephant, is considered a fine example of sculpture just a hundred years later than the Clayton Monument.

BRASSES. Most have been removed to the wall of the North Transept recently. The oldest is that of an unmarried girl with coifless hair, c.1470. The five other small brasses are the remains of larger ones, including that above the Warde memorial with which it has no connection, the Trinity in conventional form. The Warde brass is inscribed "Thoms. Warde and Jone his wyfe . . . $\overline{O}$ whos soules $\overline{JHU}$ have marcy. Ame." Warde, a prosperous tanner, who lived at Little Pendhill, died 1541 and the figures on the brass are at least fifty years earlier, so that it is probable they are pirated.

On the north side of the High Altar is a priest in Mass vestments. By his dress it dates from about 1480 and may well be Hugh Hexstall, the Rector of the Perpendicular restoration who died in 1476, but the arms are those of Ward, of Cuckfield, who have no connection with the parish. Perhaps we see more of Thomas the Tanner's pirating, for the original stone of the priest's brass can be seen in the churchyard under the south aisle wall.

THE BELLS. The fine peal of eight bells, cast by Thomas Janaway, 1780, rehung 1912, was saved from the ravages of the deathwatch beetle to ring again on Christmas Day, 1947.

THE REGISTERS date from 1538 on their original paper as ordered by Thomas Cromwell, and recently most carefully rebound. A complete transcript of the Registers, 1538-1812, is preserved in the Minet Library, Camberwell. Churchwardens' accounts date from 1546. (But see MANNING, O., and BRAY, W., History of Surrey, Vol. II, p.315.)

The list of Rectors goes back to 1293 and includes one who became Archbishop of Canterbury in 1747, Thomas Herring. The list of Churchwardens dates back to 1546.

CHURCH PLATE. An Elizabethan chalice dated 1576, and paten, which serves as a cover, dated 1566. There is a similar one at South Benfleet in Essex. A paten on a base, 1707. A flagon, "the gift of Sir William Clayton, Bart., 1733." And on the Altar a handsome pair of Venetian brass candlesticks of the 17th Century.

THE CORBELS inside the Church are worthy of note, most of them being original mediæval work, and the gargoyles on the Tower and vestry are fine workmanship of recent restorations.

Chapter IV

THE CASTLE

The castle is first mentioned in 1160 as one of the four castles in Surrey. Reigate Castle was in the hands of the de Warennes, who were in constant rivalry with the de Clares. In 1170 men from the garrison at Blechingley were sent to Canterbury to guard Archbishop Becket just before his martyrdom. In Simon de Montfort's rebellion of 1264, Gilbert de Clare, the Red Earl as he was called, sided against the King and commanded the centre of the baron's army on the field of Lewes. His castle at Tonbridge was in the King's hands and the King's son, Edward, routed the Londoners who opposed him. But Gilbert was brilliantly successful and drove the King into Lewes—Edward, like Rupert, returning from the pursuit of the Londoners, found the battle lost. The luckless Londoners were further harassed by the Royal garrison at Tonbridge and it was probably these royalist troops who, triumphant over the already defeated Londoners, marched on Blechingley Castle and captured it on their road westwards to Bristol, from where in the next year they sallied forth under the Lord Edward, who now had Gilbert de Clare as his ally, to restore the King on the field at Evesham. So ends the brief, inglorious history of Blechingley Castle, for it was dismantled and never refortified. There are earthworks and the foundations of a stone keep which date from about Stephen's reign and no doubt replaced an earlier timber structure. The name, Botteras Cross, at Barfields, preserves the site possibly of the outer defences or buttress.

Chapter V

THE BOROUGH

There is no record of when Blechingley became a borough, but no doubt it was during the early 13th Century that one of the de Clares bought the right from the King for this growing township where fulling and perhaps weaving were an increasing industry. It was never a borough under a royal charter, but a "mesne" borough, i.e. one created by its own lord with the King's permission. In 1225 occurs this assize roll: "Geoffrey Textor (weaver) is accused of theft. He was staying in the borough of Blechingley." Deeds of about this date supply us with typical names of trades and description, e.g.:

> John le Blund (the blond)
> Arnold le Cancelar (the earl's chancellor)
> John Cementar (the stonemason)
> Eustace Crulling (the curly-haired)
> William le Fleming
> Philip Giffard ("free giver" originally)
> Almer Piscator (fisher)
> Hereward Pistor (baker)
> William Faber (smith)
> Robert Isemonger (ironmonger)
> Randulph Portireve (the borough bailiff)
> William le Thume (thumb? clumsy?)
> Bartholemew le Marchaunt (merchant)
> Richard le Waleis (the Welshman)
> William Venator (the huntsman)
> Wille with-the-Fet (!)

There are also many place names, e.g. de Hamm, Hever, Horne, Stangrave, Garstone, Chivinton, Warewic.

In 1522 the borough officials were still appointed, viz. the Bailiff of the borough; the Constables, of the borough, of the "foreign" (i.e. the parish outside the borough) and of Horne; the "headboroughs" of the borough, of Horne and of Harrowsley-in-Burstow (they were the successors of the Saxon "tithing men" responsible for the peace in their area); two aletasters called Ale conners; two leather-sealers, who presumably supervised the Tannery at Pendell. The Court Leet was still functioning as a police court (besides its manorial duties) as late as 1812, when the aletasters were ordered to assay (test) the weights and measures in the borough, and in 1818 the Court fined a baker for selling bread at short weight, viz. "14 loaves each 2 oz. short."

M.P.'s. The borough did not apparently send members to
Simon de Montfort's parliament. The first recorded members were
Richard de Bodekesham and John de Geyhesham, who were returned
in 1295 to Edward I's model parliament. There is nothing very
eventful about Blechingley's representation in Parliament. Only
once was there difficulty when, in 1640, there was a disputed election
decided by the Committee of Privilege of the House. It appears
that there were 46 voters for two Members of Parliament. Blechingley was indeed a rotten borough and duly met a well-deserved
fate in 1832 when its two members disappeared. It sent two
distinguished men to Parliament just before its extinction—one was
William Lamb, in 1829, afterwards Lord Melbourne, Prime
Minister, 1834-41 and the mentor and guide of the young Queen,
and the other, the character who dominated our foreign policy for
so many years, Lord Palmerston, who voted for the Reform Bill
which removed the rotten Borough of Blechingley for which he
himself sat. As a "mesne" borough it had never had a Mayor or
Council—there was no charter—and so it ceased to exist as a
borough with the disappearance of its Members of Parliament.

THE FAIR. At Acton Burnell in 1283 Edward I granted to
Gilbert de Clare the right to have an annual fair at Blescingeleye
on the eve, feast and morrow of All Saints, and a month later
promised Gilbert the hand of his daughter Joan. The fair in the
High Street remained an annual function till modern times, but
is now sited by the Plough Inn.

CHURCH INTERIOR, LOOKING EAST

THE CHURCH FROM THE SOUTH-WEST, *c.*1797

CHAPTER VI

EARLY ENCLOSURES

CHARTLANDS. There were several patches of what we should now call "Common" in the parish. At Warwick Wood where the name "Tye" suggests open rough meadow grazing, Tilgate Heath of which only the Barfields Common remains but originally included all the golf course, and a strip right across the parish south of Castle Hill which included Sandhills, Town Farm, Michenors Bank, Coldharbour and what is now called Tilburstow Hill Plantation and Rabies Heath. Again the name "Tye" appears on the map, on Sandhills, Cuckseys and in Tye Copse. This large area has been slowly whittled away—the South Park took the southern fringe and people like Henry de Michenhale in 14th Century, Raby and Snott or Snout in 16th, to mention only a few, came to agreement with the lord of the manor and their fellow tenants to carve out their piece and fence it, until the days of enclosure acts divided up the remainder.

THE WATER MEADOWS lay along the course of the Funk Brook from Hevers Pond, across the main road by the "Plough" and along the valley past the cemetery perhaps to Ivy Mill Pond. This was originally the Lay Brook (ley=pasture clearing) and was piped in 1870 from Hevers Pond to the Cricket Field. The enclosure of the Water Meadows was perhaps started by John de Hefre, who has left his name in the parish since 1270. Walter le Finc was perhaps another encloser. He was a juror in 1232.

THE PARKS. Probably the North Park was enclosed by the earliest de Clare soon after the Conquest. In 1233 there is an order to the King's Treasurer to let Roger de Clare have 10 hinds and 2 stags to stock a park of his own. Earl Richard was a minor and the estates, therefore, in the King's hands, and it looks as if Roger, the Earl's kinsman, was starting another park. This would be the South or Great Park.

In 1262 two parks are mentioned, one of a league in circuit, the other of seven leagues. In 1296 "Parksilver" was being levied by the Red Earl to repair the park pale.

Both were "disparked" in Cromwell's time, about 1650. North Park became three farms—Hexstalls, Place Farm, and North Park. The South Park was split into six farms, two of which retain the name of South Park and the others, Cuckseys, Brownshill (now Harewoods), Gay House (by the Outwood windmills), and Lodge Farm or Gilletts in the middle of the old park. Near it can still be seen a rectangular earthwork which has been variously explained as the site of a short-lived castle in Stephen's reign, a chapel and a deer enclosure, but there is no evidence to decide the question. At South Park Farm a 17th Century building has been converted into a chapel dedicated to St. Mark.

BLECHINGLEY PLACE IN 1622, FROM WILLIAM BOYCOT'S
MAP OF PENDELL MANOR

CHAPTER VII

THE MANORS AND PARISHES

THE MANOR OF BLECHINGLEY. Granted to his cousin Richard *de Clare*, lord of Tonbridge, by William the Conqueror. The de Clares later became Earls of Hertford (1141) and Gloucester (about 1250). They played a great part in English history, especially in the reigns of Henry II, John, Henry III and the first Edward. All fought in Wales and/or France. One helped to wrest Magna Carta from King John. Another joined Simon de Montfort in overthrowing Henry III, and another restored him and supported Edward I. The last de Clare died fighting the Scots at the Battle of Bannockburn, in 1314, and his sister married

Hugh *d'Audley*, created Earl of Gloucester, 1337, and died leaving a daughter, Margaret, in 1347. She married

Ralph *de Stafford*, created Earl of Stafford. His great grandson was made Duke of Buckingham in 1444. His son was executed by Richard III, 1483, and his son, the fifth generation running to come to a bloody death, was executed by Henry VIII, in 1521, for plotting treason "in the gallery of his palace at Blechingley." The "palace" was a large house he had built of which the gatehouse only remains at Place Farm.

Henry VIII then visited Blechingley and for two years it was a royal manor before he granted it to his Master of Horse, Sir Nicholas *Carew*, K.G. He, however, fell into disfavour with his royal master and was executed in 1539.

Henry then granted Blechingley to his fourth wife, *Anne of Cleves*, whom he wished to be rid of. She seems to have spent a good deal of her time at Blechingley Place and several "Douchemen" appear in the parish registers in the years following, who were presumably her servants though almost certainly not Dutch! By the King's leave in 1547 she exchanged Blechingley for Penshurst and

Sir Thomas *Cawarden* (pronounced Carden) became lord of the manor. He was a keen Reformer and there are few local churches which escaped his zeal. Much of the church furniture, carving, rood screens, and other "idollatre" was carted to Blackfriars where, as Master of the Revels, he kept his "garnyshing." He survived Mary's reign and, dying in 1559, was buried in Blechingley Church.

Queen Elizabeth granted the manor to the younger son of the Duke of Norfolk, Lord William *Howard*, in 1561, and his more famous son was Charles, Lord Howard of Effingham, Lord High

Admiral and the Commander of the fleet which defeated the Spanish Armada. He also owned Reigate Priory, and his son, another Lord William, lived at the Place, but died before his father. The old Admiral died in 1624 and was succeeded by his granddaughter Elizabeth, who married

John, Lord *Mordaunt*, created Earl of Peterborough by Charles I. However, he supported Parliament in the Civil War, dying in 1642. His son Henry, to his mother's anger, sided with the King, and though he survived till the Restoration the estate was encumbered with debt and was sold to

Sir Robert *Clayton* in 1677. Clayton was a self-made man, chiefly by money-lending. He had already got hold of the Evelyn estates in Godstone, where he and his successors lived at Marden, and the Place, already in disrepair, was allowed to become a farm, only the Gatehouse remaining as a house. In 1835 the Claytons sold the manor to

John *Perkins*, the owner of Pendell Court, and so the two manors became united and Blechingley had again a resident lord of the manor. His sister sold to

Sir George *Maclay* in 1878, who in turn sold to

William Abraham *Bell* in 1893, whose son sold to St. Mary's Convent, Wantage, in 1947. The house is now used as a home for old people. So the Lord of the Manors of Pendhill and Blechingley is now a religious house of the English Church.

THE MANOR OF HAM. In Domesday Book Peter held it of Richard de Clare. His descendants seem to have been hereditary huntsmen to the de Clares and are variously described as de la Hamme and Venator (huntsman), or Venours, or Venars. Later it was held by the Turner family, one of whom was fined for refusing to pay Ship Money in 1638. But the 179 acres have always been detached from Blechingley and were eventually merged into the parish of Nutfield.

THE MANOR OF PENDELL. Probably not one of the three Domesday manors, but it seems to have been granted by the de Clares to the *d'Abernon* family, who left it the mediæval name of Daperons. About 1360 John *Mayu*, the then holder, sold to Sir Thomas *Uvedale*. Pendell or Daperons became the property of the younger branch of that family whose chief holdings were at Titsey and Wickham in Hampshire. About 1517 the Uvedales sold to Henry *Saunder*, of Charlwood, and after passing to the *Brends*, cousins of the Carews, the property was bought by George *Holman*, citizen and grocer of London, whose family had lived many years in Godstone. In 1624 he built the handsome house which we know as Pendell Court. His son was a Cromwellian and sat in the Parliament of 1654.

The manor passed by inheritance to the *Seyliards*, the *Scullards*, and then to the *Perkins*, by whom it was united with the Manor of

Blechingley in 1835. In 1878 Sir George Maclay, explorer and one-time Speaker of the New South Wales Parliament, bought it. He and William Bell, who bought it in 1893, added most skilfully to the house and laid out the gardens.

Close to the Court are two other handsome 17th Century houses.

PENDELL HOUSE built by Richard Glyd in 1636, Inigo Jones being traditionally the architect. The house stands on the old holding known as Schryches, after John Scriche, or sometimes Skerrett, who held it in 1495. A graceful scalloped wall erected in the 18th Century forms a courtyard on its south side and the arched entrance to this has been carried sufficiently high to allow a sedan chair to pass beneath it. A subterranean passage leading from the house under the garden down towards the river bed below may have been devised as a covered way of escape during the Civil War.

THE MANOR HOUSE so called without any justification since the Court was the manor house. In 1495 the holding was called Maldons and in the 16th Century was the tanyard of Thos. Warde. Later it became known as Little Pendell. The house was very likely built by Glyd and is certainly contemporary with Pendell House. In the 1780's it was occupied by Admiral Sir Edward Hughes, the hero of naval battles against the French Admiral de Suffren off the Indian coast.

THE MANOR OF CHEVINGTON. Civentone in Domesday was as large as Blechingley and no doubt stretched from White Hill to the forest in the south. Its western edge was probably White Post—till recently St. Catherine's Cross, and to the east it stretched to Godstone Green and actually ran along the Godstone–Caterham road north of Tyler's Green. But it was overshadowed by the Borough of Blechingley and the Walkingstead offshoot at Godstone Green and by 1262 had ceased even to be a manor. But the houses on the west of Godstone Green are even now a bone of contention between Godstone and Blechingley.

THE PARISH OF HORNE. By 1332 there was a large settlement there of some 200 people, and their names suggest that they came from many parts of the country, probably drawn by the iron smelting in the wealden forest. The church of St. Mary there dates from before this time. Horne is often treated as a separate parish, but it did not legally become so till 1705.

THE PARISH OF OUTWOOD, formed in 1870, includes part of the parish of Blechingley. The most interesting feature is the two windmills, known as the Cat and the Kitten. The Kitten is by far the older and is, in fact, one of the oldest postmills in England, being built in 1665 as it stands to-day.

CHAPTER VIII

THE VILLAGE AND ITS INSTITUTIONS

THE MARKET PLACE. This was where the War Memorial stands. There used to be a town well here, represented now by an iron pump, the sole water supply of the village until 1835. Round the corner in the High Street is the pretty old shopfront of the "Newsvendors" which, in 1800, was "Mr. Legg's the Clockmaker." The old High Street went down the narrow footpath by Selmes' Shop (it was John Selmes, Butcher, in 1740, and has been so since), past the Nicholas Woolmer cottages built in Henry VIII's reign, through Padgett's Yard (where the Church House stands. The Yard was so notorious a slum that for years the Guards at Caterham were forbidden to go there), and joined the main road by the "Plough."

INNS. The earliest inn mentioned is the "Maid," where in 1519 the churchwardens expended 3d. on entertaining the bell-ringers when Queen Catherine of Aragon passed on a visit to the Place, where she met Cardinal Wolsey. Only 2d. was spent when the King, Henry VIII, came two years later to see his new property, forfeited to him on the execution of the Duke of Buckingham. Probably the inn stood at the entrance of the village where the Red Lion now is. The royal party would turn down Parsonage Lane to the Place. Four inns are mentioned in 1704, viz. The Red Lion, The Plough, The Swan and The Bell. The first two are still with us, the "Bell" is now in Outwood, the "Swan" is the "White Hart"; several other licensed premises which sprang up at a later date have disappeared. (See Appendix III.)

The "White Hart" was probably the house of the Drake family which flourished in Blechingley for several generations. It was bought by Sir William Clayton in 1733 and probably became an inn then. From 1734 the elections, previously held at the Hall House, were held there.

BLECHINGLEY SCHOOL. In 1566 John Whatman of Crawley, mercer, one-time a native of Blechingley, gave a "messuage burgage," where the school now stands at the top of Stychens Lane (the old main road to London), "to the intent that a free school should be founded at Blechingly."

However, the school seems to have fallen into decay and became an almshouse, until it was restarted by John Evans, who lived at the Hall (where now the Village Hall stands) in 1631. His father had already given Norrey's Farm (now in Outwood) to the parish, the yearly income "to be imploid in a stock to sett the poore people on work and not to live idle." The charity still continues, so does his son's—the income from land in Nutfield Parish which enables some Blechingley children to have free scholarships.

The School is now under the County Council's control and is housed in 19th Century buildings on the site of the old foundation [D.5(7)].

THE ALMSHOUSES were built in the last century on the site of the Hall House [D.5(8)]. Older almshouses stood to the south of Court Lodge. It is possible that the manor courts were sometimes held at Court Lodge, which is a 16th-century house.

THE VILLAGE HALL AND CLUB, started in the last century, are amongst the best in the county. There is a good stage and the Hall has an excellent dancing floor [D.5(8)].

THE CHURCH HOUSE, built early in this century, blocks the old High Street just south of the Church. There are two rooms available for use; the County Library is held there [E.5(11)].

There is a children's playing field beside the School and a handsome cricket ground opposite the Plough Inn, known as Grange Meadow.

North of the Church is a large Institution run by the County Council called Clerk's Croft [E.5].

CHAPTER IX

SOME LOCAL NAMES

Barfields. As "Burrfields" it appears in 1680, and may refer to local stone which in 18th Century was called "burr"; "four wads of burr" were used to repair the churchyard wall in 1750. There was a Richard Burre in Blechingley in the 16th Century, or it may just be a corruption of Barnfield [D.5].

Belcroft. Belacre, 1229. In 1546 Sackville as owner of Belcroft paid a yearly rent of 1s. to the churchwardens for bellropes and it was sold in 1586 subject to this charge. In 1753 a workhouse was built on it but it has remained church property and is now the site of Clerk's House beside Selme's shop [DE.5].

Bewells. On Town Farm now being dug away for sand, possibly preserves the name of Eustace de Buell of 1215, or more probably the Bowells who appear in the church register in late 16th Century [E.6].

Blackbushes, above Pendell, first appears in 1451 and has remained ever since [D.2].

Boterys Cross. Barfields Road used to continue south of the main road down the hill. In 1527 Thos. Lambe was in trouble for allowing roots to obstruct the road. The name possibly is Buttridge, or boundary ridge, crossroads, or more likely preserves the site of some outer defence, or buttress, of the Castle [D.5].

Brewerstreet, more commonly Brewhouse until recently, but it is not a very old name, first appearing in 1608. (See under *Hexstall*) [DE.3].

Brownshill, one of the five South Park farms, now Harewoods. John Browne was tenant in 1704 [E.10].

Cacketts, or *Kecketts*—the field immediately north of Snats Hill, next door to Rabbits Heath Cottage. The Cachett family lived in Blechingley from 1555 till 1738 [G.5].

Catherine's Cross, now known as White Post, where no doubt a shrine of St. Catherine stood at the road junction. The new housing estate has revived the name [E.5].

Chapel Plat near Lodge Farm, a roughly quadrangular moated enclosure, is clearly marked. It has never been properly excavated but mediæval pottery and a fine Bronze Age hone have been found (*v.* S.A.C. XXXVI, p.112) [F.9].

A ROOF-CORBEL IN THE CHURCH

Cockley, originally common land where the Pest House was built in Tudor times. The wood was planted after 1814. The name, Cockley or Cocknam, appears here in 1577, but no one of that name is known to be connected there. The Common was enclosed in 1812 [C.4].

Coldharbour cannot be traced further than 1741 in records; previously it was part of Rabies. The name had a vogue of popularity from 14th to 18th Century and is common in almost every county. It probably means exactly what it says, a shelter from the cold [F.6].

Cuckseys, the Cuxey or Cucksey family were tenants of the Claytons for most of the 18th Century and gave their name to one of the farms of the South Park [F.7].

Funk. Funk's Bridge carried the road over the Laybrook (q.v.) by the Plough Inn. The name Funkmead appears in 1527 and possibly recalls Walter le Finc, a juror in 1262, or Walter Funke, whose name appears in Blechingley in 1332. (The word originally was connected with spark or fire. In the 17th Century it began to suggest stink from connection with tobacco, but the connection with fear is not found till the 18th Century) [E.5, F.4].

Furlongsfield, 1761, behind the Institution, recalls one of the Common Fields of mediæval days where the villagers held their strips of arable land, 220 yards long by a cricket pitch wide [E.4].

Garston (often spelt and probably pronounced locally Garson or Gasson) is one of the oldest names in the Parish. It may possibly be "Goers-tun," the grassy enclosure, or from "Goers" sandstone, but more probably came with the family William de Garston who bought the land in 1229, and coming from one of the many Garstons in England brought the name with him. The last member of the family is recorded in 1364, Roger atte Garstone. The estate was for a long period reputed a manor [G.5].

Glenfield. The Georgian front hides a much older building. It was long the house of the Sargant family. The name Glenfield is modern [DE.5(5)].

The Grange. A modern name. Originally the farmhouse of Town Farm. In the 16th Century it was occupied by the Hoskins family, who later built Barrow Green in Oxted, where their descendants still live. In the 17th Century it was occupied by the Drakes, and later by the Russells, but the Hoskins sold it in 1738. Since 1866 a doctor has lived there (See Town Farm) [E.5(1)].

Harewoods. v. Brownshill.

Hangdog's Wood, the south-east corner of the parish east of Lower South Park, now treated as Blindley Heath. Probably derived from one of the Dodds—tenants of Lower South Park whose nickname was "Hen" [G.10].

Henhaw, the south-west corner of the parish near Crabhill, South Nutfield, a more recent name for Lepars (q.v.) [C.8].

Hevers. A very ancient name brought by a family from Hever in Kent in the 13th Century. John, Stephen and Gilbert de Hefre were witnesses in about 1250. John and Joan de Hever swapped some land, probably this, in 1271. Nicholas de Hevere held land in Blecchyngeleghe in 1313 [E.6].

Hexstall. The name comes to the parish about 1447 when Thomas Hexstalle was M.P., as was William in 1450, while in 1451 Hugh was presented by the Duke of Buckingham to the living and remained Rector for 25 years. It is safe to assume that the Hexstalls had built a house which later bore their name and farmed land in and around North Park. It is likely that the Hermitage marks the site of the old Hexstall house. These four brothers came from Staffordshire; William was mixed up in Jack Cade's rebellion of 1450. Henry quite likely built the fine half-timbered house which used to be known as Le Venars or the Tan House (a name also used of what is now the Manor House) and now Brewer Street Farm. The family disappears from Blechingley in the reign of Henry VIII [E.2].

Holloway—the old lane leading west from Place Farm and originally turning south behind Brewer Street to join Sandy Lane west of the Old Rectory. Richard atte Holeweye was a juror in 1297. It ceased to be used when Carwarden and the churchwardens set out the new road linking Brewer Street with Sandy Lane in front of the Old Rectory in 1550 [D.3].

Ironlatch Field, 1841, name of field south of Whitepost where the new Council cottages are being built. Presumably refers to the gate fastening. It was originally part of Scrouches (q.v.) [EF.5].

Isemongers, now Water House. A tenant's name in 1328 and the name remained as Icemonger or Eyesmonger till the 18th Century. (Ironmonger.) [F.4].

Joon Roses, a house settled by John Bridgell on his wife in 1505. It stood on the east side of Brewer Street between Old Rectory and Place Farm, possibly one of the cottages still standing there. It seems an early example of a fancy name [D.4].

Laybrook. A stream used to run north from Hevers Pond which is fed by a spring, crossing the now main road by Funk's Bridge, east of the Plough Inn, and thence north of the Cemetery to Ivy Mill Pond. It was piped by Mr. Perkins about 1850. Lay=ley, clearing or meadow [E.5].

Lepars. A road went due south down the hill from Barfields, Bottery's Cross to Unwyns, Grays, Tunbrig, Lepars, and crossed the line of the railway to Henhaw and Doghurst. Lepars first appears in 1458. In 1527 Thomas Lambe was summoned for allowing trees to obstruct the lane. In 1704 it is still called Lepars, but more recently has been corrupted into Leopards. It probably recalls some long-forgotten tenant [CD.7].

Le Lords Field, 1523, owned by Richard Stevens and subsequently by the Evans and the Drakes. It is now represented by Tower House and garden. The name doubtless implies that it was once part of the "demesne" land [E.5(3)].

Manor House—really "Maldons," left by Henry Hexstall to his wife in 1493. Mistress Katherine Maldon was the tenant of a house by Pendell Marsh, now the lake, from 1451-95 and there seems little doubt that she left her name to the house which stood where the so-called Manor House now stands. The present house was most probably built by Glyd and called Little Pendhill [C.4].

Middle Row, 1680, the houses on the south side of the old High Street forming an island when the new High Street was made. One of the cottages is called King Charles' Cottage because certain leases of it were found of that date [E.5(11)].

Mint. Possibly where the village tradesmen's tokens were struck in and after Oliver Cromwell's days. (The Presbyterian constable, Joseph Buttery, was still issuing tokens in 1666. Richard Miles at the "Grocer's Arms" also issued tokens, two of which survive, dated 1656 and 1665. No copper coinage was minted by the Government till 1672 and tokens were then forbidden.) [E.5(11)].

Michenalls (or *Mitchenors*). The farmhouse has disappeared by the lane from Hevers to Coldharbour but the bank still retains the name. The foundations of the farm can be traced at the foot of the bank. The name derives from Henry de Michenale in 1347 [E.6].

Motherips, field south of the railway immediately west of Poundhill Bridge. The name appears in 1841 Tithe Map just when the railway was being built and it may preserve the memory of the "muddy cuts" from the wheeling of the navvies' barrows [D.7].

Norbryght's Hole, north-east corner of South Park, just south of Underhills. The name really belongs to Godstone Parish and is of Saxon origin—"north clearing" or "bright spot" [G.7].

Old Rectory. An attractive 18th century front masks an old house probably of the 16th century.

Onions Hole, north of Sandhills, a valley leading up to Outwood Lane opposite Hevers Sandpit gate, probably recalls Thos. Onyon, a tenant in 1694 [DE.6].

Parker's Corner, 22-acre pasture almost opposite Burstow Park gate in the Outwood Lane. A John le Parker was concerned in 1301 with many others in a raid on property in Chipstead when they cut John de Beauchamp's corn and drove off 200 sheep. The following year Thos. le Parker, also of "Blechingeleye," was imprisoned at Reigate Castle for poaching on a grand scale. Perhaps the name recalls this notorious family, or it may be just a meeting-place of the park keepers from Burstow and South Park [E.9].

Parkgate Cottages, in Outwood Lane—modern cottages mark the old main entrance to South Park from the Castle [E.7].

Parsonage Lane. One of the oldest highroads in the parish. Starting from Castle Square it leads past the school, down Stichens, to join the present road at Brewerstreet. There were constant complaints at the Manor Court about roots and rocks obstructing this deep hollow lane and it was finally closed by Quarter Sessions in 1803. It is now only a footpath and the lane has long been used as a rubbish tip [D.4-5].

Pendell, la Pende, 1259, Pendhull in Sir Thos. Uvedale's will 1367, Pendhill 1451, Pendchyll 1522. Doubtless a Saxon name, Pen=enclosure, in some of the richest land of early settlement. The modern suggestion of "dell" is obvious for reason of its position but it is fairly clear its origin was rather in "hill" than "dell" [CD.3].

Pest House, on the east side of the old golf course. A Tudor house in origin and the village "Isolation" hospital, standing on common land till the enclosure of 1812. In 1732 it was ruinous and had to be repaired. Now called Cockley Cottage [C.4].

Pightle or *Pickles*, a small close or field, appears in several places in 1761 and 1841 Tithe Maps at Sandhills, on Coldharbour and on the Glebe land. The "i" is really long and the word denotes "enclosure."

Pottersgate, 1517, the north entrance to the South Park where the road originally from North Park comes over the hill, past Underhills and enters the South Park. There are signs of clay ponds for brick and tile works nearby [G.7].

Pound Farm, between Chevingtons and Rabies Heath, probably marks the site of the pound for impounding stray animals on the manor of Chevington. Blechingley Pound stood just south of Lacroix's shop [G.5].

Poundhill, just south of the railway on Outwood Lane. The name recalls the pound or hammer used in iron smelting, a common industry here and in Sussex before the Industrial Revolution, cf. Cinderhill beside it. The wood was planted some time before 1700 by Sir Robert Clayton to supply his powder mills at Godstone. (The Evelyns of Wotton, Dorking, Marden and Leigh Place in Godstone were granted a monopoly of gunpowder making in the south by Queen Elizabeth, and Sir Robert had foreclosed on a mortgage and so got the Evelyn estates which included a good deal of Blechingley land.) [E.8].

Prestwell, 1451, originally part of Town Farm, now partly the Isolation Hospital land, but the old house, now called Brickkiln, stands in Tilburstow Lane. The name is derived from Priest wall or well [F.5].

Puckmire Field, 1841, on Harewoods—a wet, muddy field where calves were apt to get "the puck" or quarter-ill.

Pulterscroft, 1499, a field on the Nutfield boundary by Pendell Mill. Roger le Poletor was bailiff to the Red Earl in 1290 and John Poletor, a juror in 1307. The name appears again in the parish in 1661. Perhaps it marks the site of an early chicken farm [C.4].

Pynok Hill, Pynnockeshelde juxta Blessyngelegh, 1294. In 1526 the sale of Pynakeshele is recorded in the Manor Court. Perhaps the name recalls a former de Clare tenant, Nicholas de Pinnux, who came from Pinnock in Gloucestershire. In 1680 Pendix Hill and 1841 Penduck Shaw appears for the same piece of ground—the hill on the south of Tilburstow Lane often called Windy Gap stretching west to Snatts Hill [G.6].

Rabies Heath, to the south of the Tilburstow Road, was common land, the East Chart, until the enclosure act of 1814 : Pound Farm was on the north and Rabeys below Snatts Hill, now on Cold-harbour, probably marks the original holding of John Rabie in 1527. The Rabies also held Wychefelde (now Underhills) and most of Coldharbour and left their name to the Common to the north of them on the Greensand bank. Parishioners still have the right to dig gravel "for purposes of husbandry" on the Heath. There is an inevitable modern corruption to Rabbits Heath [FG.6].

Sackville Cottages, 14 paired cottages built in 1921 by the R.D.C. just south of Town Farm. The name recalls the 16th Century owner [E.5].

Sandhills. In 1529 the Manor Court directed that the inhabitants "shall raise and mend the road from Sandhills to le South Parke gate, which was founderous, before Pentecost." The farm was called Napletons and in 1738 was sold to Sir Daniel Lambert, whose descendants built the present house about 1870 [D.6].

Long Scrouches, the 70-acre arable field to the south of Whitepost where the R.D.C. are building new houses. John Scroucher appears in a 12th Century deed, possibly John of St. Crouch, the holy crossway where stood the shrine of St. Catherine, now known as Whitepost [E.5].

Sharpsfield or *Sharpsland*, in 1522 Sharpsriden—roden or rutting (as in Essex)—the land enclosed from forest and cultivated. Great Sharps, as it is now called, is a 24-acre field which the footpath from the Old Rectory to the church crosses. It must have been on the Common Field—a wet, alder-growing spot till perhaps reclaimed by Roger Sharp, bailiff to the Red Earl in 1290 [DE.4].

Shawls, 1704, immediately north of Poundhill railway bridge the cottage garden and foundations can still be seen. A "shawl" is a kneading trough, but it may simply recall a tenant's name. The cottages and barn were pulled down to build Sandhills [E.7].

Shriches, "a croft opposite the cross." The name appears after 1451 as Schiches, Schryches, Schirches and Scrichys. In 1520 it is described as the croft opposite the cross now decayed. The cross probably stood on the high ground in front of Glyd's house, now Pendell House, and was probably the market cross of Pendell which never became a proper market. After Glyd built his house the name disappears.

Snatts, 1522, a holding on the south side of Tilburstow Lane which seems to have been an enclosure on the common land of Rabies Heath. The Lambe family held it from before 1519 till after 1704, when it is referred to as Snots. A Belgian artist, Campo Tosto, built a studio and house there which still keeps the name, as does the hill down to Underhills and South Park. The name probably recalls Walter Snoute, a juror in 1343 and 1347 [G.6].

Spinns Barn. Spynes 1841, Speens 1704, a holding south of Merstham Road, opposite Coppice Lea. Spind is Anglo-Saxon for fat and the name may refer to the rich valley land [B.3].

Stangrave. Ivy House has recently reverted to this old name brought from Stonegrave in the North Riding before 1250. They were important tenants of the de Clares; John de Stangrave was the Earl's seneschal in 1258 and his grandson, Robert, Lord of the Manor of Edenbridge, was caught poaching the Archbishop's deer at Malling in 1285. He was made a knight on the field of Caerlaverock in 1300 by Edward I. He was, in 1307, "Knight of the Shire" (M.P.) and, later, Sheriff of Surrey, and in 1326 he had a licence for a chapel in his house. His son became Lord of Oxted Manor, but when he died in 1360 he left no son, and shortly afterwards Stangrave passed to the de Staffords and so merged with Blechingley. Subsequently, it was held by the Barbour family, the Beechers, and from 1672 the Northeys. We have a detailed instruction for the rebuilding of Ivy Mill in 1680 when for £40 Charles Ridley, Carpenter of Blechingley, undertook to build a house 33 feet by 16 feet with a central chimney stack and four rooms besides outbuildings. We can see the house to-day, although a recent fire has done damage. Thomas Northey pulled down the Tudor house at Stangrave in 1740 and renamed his new home Ivy House [G.4].

Stocklands, a holding lying to north and south of the Pendell–Merstham Road and west of Warwick Wood. Robert atte Stokke was a manor tenant in 1336. The stock was a trough used for fulling cloth. In 1493 Stocklands is mentioned as being left by Henry Hextall to his wife. In the 18th Century it belonged to the

PENDELL COURT

BREWERSTREET FARM

Evelyns, one of whom founded a school at Felbridge which was endowed with an annual charge of £21 on Stocklands. This was eventually discharged by the owner of Oakley [B.2-3].

Stychens, Stiche, 1434 (Stychell, 1523). The name is preserved in the cottage built by Mr. Perkins before 1840 north of the school and is derived from the "stycce" (pieces) or "lands" of the Common Field [DE.4-5],

Tanhouse. In 1517 Thomas Warde held the Tanhouse at the annual rent of 2s. The remains of it can quite likely be seen in the garden wall of Little Pendhill (the Manor House.) (But see "Hexstalls.")

Thomasland, 1520, the park to the south of Pendell Court [CD.4].

Tilgate. What was later known as Blechingley Common, derived from either "till," rough ground, or "thill," shafts of a cart, cf. Tilburstow, which may be the "buster" or bridge which would carry wheeled traffic—a rare occurrence [C.4-5].

Tower House, built about 1860 on the old holding known as "le lord's field" (q.v.) [E.5(3)].

Town Farm. Sackville property in Henry VIII's time from which the north chimney stack probably dates. It was owned by the Hoskins family of Oxted, 1586-1767. In 1866 the house became separated from the farm and is now known as the Grange (q.v.) [E.5(1, 2)].

Tye. The name appears in three places in the parish: on the northern boundary by Warwick Wood; at Sandhills, as a field name; and at South Park, where the large covert planted by the Claytons in 18th Century beside the Pottersgate is called Tye Copse. Tye means common pasture for rough grazing. The name is an old one and can be associated with William de la Theighe and Turstan de la Tye, 1241 [C.2, D.6, F.7].

Tylers Green—in the parish of Godstone, but the manor of Blechingley, recalls the name of a family who lived there in Henry VIII's time. Benet, son of Nicholas and Filys Tyler, was christened in 1539. The Green was enclosed in 1810 [H.3].

Underhills was long the name of Castle Hill Farm for obvious reasons—1523 and down to modern times. In 1870 Mr. Warren Smith built a house at Wychcroft (or Prickloves Farm as it was called sometimes (*e.g.* 1819). Both these names were lost and the name Underhills is now used by the Farm Training College there [D.5, G.7].

Unwyns, a holding south of the Castle. The name appears in 1527: held by the Cholmeleys, Gainsfords and Drakes, but since 1841 merged into Castle Hill property. Probably preserves the name of the Onion family and there is no trace of a Saxon origin (Unwyn=unfriendly in A.S.) [D.6].

War Coppice. Now the name of a private house on White Hill, but of ancient origin and recalls the prehistoric camp site of which there are traces. Possibly connected with our word "ward"— defence [E.2].

Warwick Wood, at the north-west corner of the parish. A William de Warewic appears in 1225, and Giles atte Warc was a tenant in 1340. The name preserves this connection or possibly is related to the prehistoric camp site nearby (*v.* War Coppice). The name Warwick Wode appears in 1528 and the common there was enclosed in 1810. It is often called Warwick Wold nowadays, but this has no historical basis [C.2].

Water House. v. Isemongers.

Wellers. A holding north of Pendell Court, it was also called Bennets; both recall tenants' names. Weller was a family in 17th Century. Now pulled down [D.3].

Whitepost. v. Catharine's Cross.

Wilcox or *Wilcock.* North-west corner of the parish west of Warwick Wood. Probably preserves the name of Thos. Wilcotes and John Wycotys, who were M.P.'s for Blechingley in 1449 and 1460 [B.2].

Windmill Fields mark the site of the lord's mill on the south side of the main road beside Woolpits [CD.5].

Wolkested Barn, a cottage which stood where now the new cottages stand on the north side of Godstone Green. It was just on the parish boundary, but the Manor of Blechingley reached to the London–Eastbourne Road and included Needles Bank. Wolkested or Walking Stead was the old name for Godstone and the Saxon village stood round St. Nicholas' Church. (Walking= fulling)—the settlement on the Roman road was a later development [G.4].

Wolmer's Cottages, in the old High Street, built 1552 by Nicholas Wolmer, on waste land of the Manor granted at the Court Baron for a fine of 8d. and a rent of 2d. [E.5(10)].

Woolpits, actually in Nutfield parish, but part of the holding in 1738 was assessed under Blechingley. Probably old sandpits used for shearing sheep in [C.5].

APPENDIX I

THE DESCENT OF THE MANORS

DE CLARES, d'AUDLEY, STAFFORD

Richard the Fearless, Duke of Normandy
d. 996

Richard the Good, Duke of Normandy

Robert the Devil, Duke of Normandy

WILLIAM THE CONQUEROR
Duke of Normandy
and King of England

Godfrey, Count of Brionne

Gilbert, Count of Brionne
murdered 1040

Richard, Lord of Clare and Tonbridge
(granted Blechingley by
William the Conqueror)
Justiciar of England 1073, d. 1090

Gilbert de Clare
Was with William Rufus when he
was shot in New Forest, d. 1115

Richard de Clare
Killed fighting for King in Wales, 1136

Gilbert de Clare
1st Earl of Hertford
o.s.p., 1141

Roger de Clare
2nd Earl of Hertford
Quarrelled with Thos. à Becket, d. 1173

Richard de Clare
3rd Earl of Hertford
Helped to force King John to seal Magna Carta,
d. 1217

Gilbert de Clare
4th Earl of Hertford
1st Earl of Glo'ster
also sealed Magna Carta,
d. 1230

Henry III
d. 1272

Edward I
d. 1307

Richard de Clare
5th Earl of Hertford
2nd Earl of Glo'ster
Adviser to Henry III
d. 1262

Edward II   Joan   =   Gilbert de Clare ("The Red Earl")
d. 1327   6th Earl of Hertford
                                            3rd Earl of Glo'ster
Sided with Simon de Montfort, won Battle of Lewes,
1264, but later rescued the King, d. 1295

29

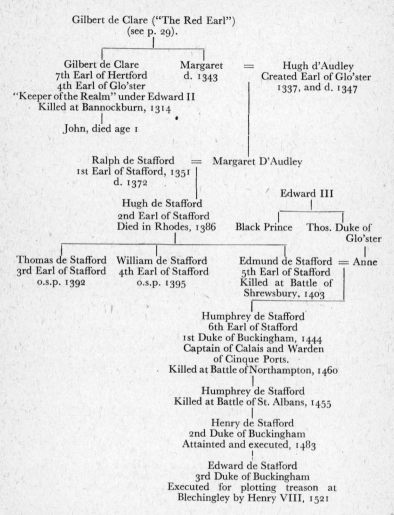

Gilbert de Clare ("The Red Earl")
(see p. 29).

Gilbert de Clare   Margaret   =   Hugh d'Audley
7th Earl of Hertford   d. 1343   Created Earl of Glo'ster
4th Earl of Glo'ster   1337, and d. 1347
"Keeper of the Realm" under Edward II
Killed at Bannockburn, 1314

John, died age 1

Ralph de Stafford   =   Margaret D'Audley
1st Earl of Stafford, 1351
d. 1372

Edward III

Hugh de Stafford
2nd Earl of Stafford
Died in Rhodes, 1386   Black Prince   Thos. Duke of
                                           Glo'ster

Thomas de Stafford   William de Stafford   Edmund de Stafford   =   Anne
3rd Earl of Stafford   4th Earl of Stafford   5th Earl of Stafford
o.s.p. 1392   o.s.p. 1395   Killed at Battle of
                                       Shrewsbury, 1403

Humphrey de Stafford
6th Earl of Stafford
1st Duke of Buckingham, 1444
Captain of Calais and Warden
of Cinque Ports.
Killed at Battle of Northampton, 1460

Humphrey de Stafford
Killed at Battle of St. Albans, 1455

Henry de Stafford
2nd Duke of Buckingham
Attainted and executed, 1483

Edward de Stafford
3rd Duke of Buckingham
Executed for plotting treason at
Blechingley by Henry VIII, 1521

Henry VIII then granted the land to Sir Nicholas Carew, his Master of Horse. He was executed in 1539.

Henry VIII then granted it to Anne of Cleeves, who in 1547 exchanged Blechingley for Hever Castle and Sir. Thos. Cawarden came here. His executors sold to the Howards.

THE HOWARDS AND MORDAUNTS

Thomas Howard
2nd Duke of Norfolk
Victor of Flodden, d. 1524

Dukes of Norfolk

Lord William Howard
Lord Admiral 1553
Created 1st Baron Howard of Effingham
for suppressing Wyatt's Rebellion, 1554
Granted Blechingley, 1560, d. 1573

Charles Howard
2nd Baron Howard of Effingham
Lord Admiral 1585
Defeated Armada 1588
Created Earl of Nottingham, 1596
d. 1624, age 87

Lord William Howard
d. 1615

John Lord Mordaunt   =   Elizabeth Howard
Created Earl of Peterborough
by Charles I. He supported Parlt.
in the Civil War and died 1642

Henry Mordaunt
2nd Earl of Peterborough
Supported the King and lost a great
deal of money. In 1677 he had to
sell the property to pay his debts.

THE CLAYTONS

Sir Robert Clayton
Born at Bulwick, Northants, 1629
(His father was a carpenter)
Apprenticed to his uncle a scrivener
in London. Lord Mayor, 1679
M.P. for Blechingley, d. 1705
He lived at Marden in Godstone

Thomas Clayton

Sir William Clayton
Created 1732 1st Baronet.
M.P. for Blechingley

Sir Kenrick Clayton
2nd Baronet
M.P. for Blechingley, 1734-1769,
d. 1769

Sir Robert Clayton
3rd Baronet
M.P. for Blechingley
o.s.p. 1799

William Clayton
of Harlingford, Bucks

Sir William Clayton
4th Baronet, married Mary,
dau. of Sir Wm. East of
Hall Place, Maidenhead

Sir William Clayton
5th Baronet
Wounded at Quatrebras,
fought at Waterloo.
A General 1865, d. 1866
Sold Manor to J. Perkins in 1835

A BUTCHER'S ACCOUNT-BOOK

The Blechingley butcher's shop has been kept by the Selmes family for over two centuries, and some of the earlier accounts are still preserved. We are indebted to Mr. William Selmes for permission to give some information about them. There are 18 leaves of accounts kept by Philip Puttock, of Godstone, in 1770-73, but more noteworthy is a book, size 15in. by 6in., bound in vellum, and containing accounts kept by Mr. John Selmes from 1783 to 1802. Unfortunately, few book customers were Blechingley people, but the record is interesting for prices and for the light thrown on the consumption of different types of meat. Pork seldom occurs, but "hine Qr." was 9d. a lb. in 1788, and "Loyn Porke" was 5¾d. a year later. Lamb, a common meat at the beginning of the book, was not sold at all by 1802, possibly on account of food scarcity in the Napoleonic War. The chief prices were :—

					1783	1802
Beef	...	...	...	...	2½-5d.	8½d.
Mutton	...	...	...	...	5d.	8½d.
Veal	...	...	...	...	5d.	9d.
Lamb	...	...	...	...	3d.	—

The consumption of meat was considerable : in the month of December, 1801, John Brown, wheelwright, spent £1 0s.8d. on 22 lbs. of mutton and 5½ lbs. of beef, while in December, 1793, Sir Robert Clayton's household consumed 88 stone 8 lbs. of beef and veal, with two calf's feet and "Shinn Calves Head and Runnet" to a total cost of £16 14s.0d. ; in May, 1800, the Workhouse had 21 stone 4½ lbs. of beef, and 25 lbs. "Suit," costing £5 16s.1½d. Mr. Cole, who seldom ate beef, bought 73 lbs. of mutton and lamb, and a "Ligg Vel" in four days, in May, 1784. John Perkins, Esq., apparently to work off arrears of rent owed to him by Mr. Selmes, had 1s.4d. worth of tripe weekly for the two years 1801-02. Mr. Thomas Pawley owed a bill of £378 in 1799, when he went bankrupt, but most of it had been recovered by 1807. The Rev. Mr. Goodricks spent some £2 10s.0d. every six weeks ; in 1800 the Rev. Mr. Beresford's Christmas ration was 23 lbs. of "Rostg. Beef and Suit" costing 17s.3d., instead of his normal allowance of 3s. or 4s. a week.

There are some pleasant spellings : "Middereffmeat," "Bladlers," and "Ligg," and incidentals include the frequent payments by Mr. John Sex of 6¼d. for a letter, and £1 8s.2d. for newspapers in 1802.

THE VILLAGE IN 1816

We can recapture a fairly clear idea of Blechingley residents about 130 years ago, thanks to the Churchwardens' accounts and an informative conveyance of a large number of houses in the Borough by William Kenrick to Matthew Russell in 1816.

In 1811 there were 184 houses in the parish of which 96 were in the borough. The total population was 1,116 souls, males predominating by about 30 over females.

The old main road had already long been blocked and the present high-road opened. But the village was not so very different in appearance. Castle Hill, Blechingley House, the present Rectory, Brittan's Cottages on the Bank, the Almshouses and the Village Hall were not to be seen. The site of the Hall was occupied by a rather ramshackle three-gabled building known as the Hall House, owned in 1816 jointly by John Radley and William Istead. John Radley himself lived at Tilgates which was sold at his death in 1822, and it looks as if the Hall House was used as cottages.

The White Hart, referred to as "3 messuages used as one house," was bought by the Claytons in 1733 from John Jewell and Jane, his wife. In 1816 it is referred to as "formerly the Swan" and in the occupation of Ralph Eldridge who had recently succeeded his father, James. Ralph supplied Communion wine, "ringers' ale" (quite a large annual item after the reinstatement of the bells in 1780 and increased even more by the occasions of the cleaning of the fire engine kept in the church tower) and port for the paupers at the churchwardens' expense. In 1816 he was paid £3 18s.6d. for refreshment for the Bishop and servants at Confirmation. Next year a similar sum, "for four at Confirmation." James Eldridge was then churchwarden. This year saw the stocks used at Blechingley for the last recorded time. The constable was paid 2s.6d. for "summonsing Barber's wife and putting her in the stocks." In 1821 the churchwardens paid Ralph "2s.4d. for 4 gals. of ale for the men that killed the mad dog."

The Cottage of Content "in front of the Almshouses" was occupied by Thomas Best, William Wren lived next door and next to him James Agate. James Hale and Thomas Best apparently had the tenancy of the blacksmith's shop and Henry Wallis lived on the corner of Workhouse Lane. Bird's shop was Thomas Chapman, hairdresser: the Mint, Widow Roffey and Richard Smith: the garage, Simon Shepherd, plumber. Between the garage and post office a house had recently been removed to make a better approach to the church—the "Great Alley" as opposed to the Little Alley in Middle Row. Where Church House now stands Charles Wood lived.

In Church Walk, the house on the corner of the churchyard was formerly the "One Bell," now divided into two, occupied by —Brown and Abraham Brown. Next door the two cottages were occupied by William Dove and Thomas Winchester. This house was bought by the Claytons in 1696. The butcher's shop then as now was John Selmes.

In Middle Row, the post office and the cottage to the west were occupied by Anthony Finch and John Burnall. The house now known as King Charles Cottage was formerly a public house called the Angel and Crown, then the Green Dragon and more recently the Coach and Horses, lately occupied by William Charman and in 1816 by Martin Bray. The Jewells had sold this house and the one to the east to the Claytons in 1732. Long-hurst's shop is recorded as being formerly called "Toodhams" and later was called the "Newsvendors"; this shop is described as being next "the Town Well" and occupied by John Legg, the clockmaker.

On the south side of the main road it is a little difficult to identify all the houses with certainty. Of the cottages which stood where the Bank Buildings are now—one was apparently called "Mole Pits," another was occupied by Peter Swelling and another by Widow Callister, and John Newbury held the field known as Lordsfield—Tower House garden. The Grange was Robert Webb, surgeon; Oxstall, Charles Inwood and the house now the Prince Albert was Widow Warbourne.

There is a house called Ashleys which may be one of those to the west of Glenfield occupied by Edward Russell. It looks as though John Skinner and John Dalton lived at Glenfield as it is now called, and the old shop next door was occupied by James Withers, William Feliwood and Richard Norman.

In the east part of the borough, the Red Lion, previously the Angel and before that probably the Maid, was occupied by William Kent. The Manse was occupied by John Steel and there were some cottages opposite up Stychens Lane tenanted by Widow Newbury, James Roots, Thomas Pain and Thomas Holland. One of these may have been Castle Cottage. Thomas Webb, chemist, was another tenant there who may have occupied the present chemist's shop. Masterton's shop was apparently a butcher's kept by Thomas Holland, junior. Benjamin Matthews lived on the south side of the street and John Cawley and Thomas Risbridger were tenants at the Blechingley House stables.

Identification of the houses between the School and Selmes is difficult. Robert Roffey lived by the school, then Stephen

Feldwick and Stephen Ackhurst possibly at Poplar House, while
Robert Mayne, Richard Borer, John Martingale, William Laing,
and William Bridger occupied houses between that and the Hall
House.

The main interest of this deed is that it is an excellent example
of the control of a rotten borough in the unreformed parliament.
The Claytons were gradually buying control from 1682 until
about 1750. From then on the Kenricks were buying the control
from the Claytons, but now in 1816 the procedure has been
simplified and by this conveyance Mathew Russell of Brancepeth
Castle, Co. Durham, buys nearly all the property in the borough
and so the control of two members of parliament. He was duly
elected M.P. for Blechingley in 1818, but he only sat for a few
months as he was also elected for Saltash, Cornwall. William
Russell, his son, sat for a few months as member for Blechingley
in 1826, and was succeeded by William Lamb, the future Prime
Minister. Six years later the Reform Act swept away Blechingley's
two members of Parliament.

SEAL OF GILBERT DE CLARE, LAST EARL OF GLOUCESTER.
KILLED AT BANNOCKBURN, 1314

INDEX

ABERNON, D', family, 16
Ackhurst, Stephen, 36
Agate, James, 34
Almshouses, 19
Andred, forest, 5
Aragon, Catherine of, 18
Audley, Hugh d', 15, App. I.

BACON, John, jnr., 9
Baker, Hereward the, 11
Bank Buildings, 35
Barbour, family, 26, 34
Barfield, 20
Beauchamp, John de, 23
Becket, Archbishop, 10
Beecher, family, 26
Belcroft, 20
Bell, family, 16, 17
Bells, church, 9
Bennets v. Wellers
Bensley, Sir William, 9
Beresford, Rev. Mr., 33
Best, Thomas, 34
Bewells, 20
Biscoe, J. S., 9
Blackbushes, 20
Blechingley, name, 3 ; manor, 15
Bodekesham, Richard de, 12
Bordars, 4, 5
Borer, Richard, 36
Borough, ch. V.
Boterys, 20
Boundaries, 5
Boycot, William, 14
Brasses, 9
Bray, Martin, 35
Brend, family, 16
Brewerstreet, 20
Bridgell, John, 22
Bridger, William, 36
Brown, family, 35
Browne, John, 20

Brownshill, 20
Buckingham, Dukes of, 7, 18, App. I.
Buell, Eustace de, 20
Burnall, John, 35
Burre, Richard, 20
Buttery, Joseph, 23

CACKETTS, 20
Callister, Widow, 35
Carew, Sir Nicholas, 15
Castle, ch. IV., 4
— Cottage, 35
Catherine's, St., Chapel of, 7 ; Cross, 17, 20, 25
Cawarden, Sir Thomas, 8, 15
Cawley, John, 35
Cell, hermit's, 7
Chapel, 7, 14
— Plat, 20
Chapman, Thomas, 34
Charman, William, 35
Chevington, 3, 4, 5
Cholmeley, family, 27
Church, ch. III
— House, 19
Churchwardens' Account, 34
Clare, de, family, 15, App. I.
Clare, Gilbert de, 10
Clare, Richard de, 4
Clare, Roger de, 13
Clayton, Monument, 8 ; lord of manor, 16, App. I ; butcher's account, 33, v. App. III.
Clayton, Sir Robert, 16, 24, 33
Clayton, Sir William, 9, 18
Cleves, Anne of, 9, 15
Cockley, 21, 24
Coldharbour, 21
Court Lodge, 19
Crutcher, Richard, 8
Cuckseys, 13, 21

37

BIDDLES LTD
PRINTERS
GUILDFORD